HEROKEE

TELL ME WHY, TELL ME HOW

# HOW DO TORNADOES FORM?

## RENEE C. REBMAN

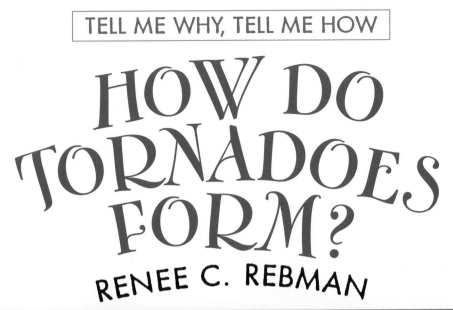

 **Marshall Cavendish**
Benchmark
New York

Published by Marshall Cavendish Benchmark
An imprint of Marshall Cavendish Corporation

This publication represents the opinions and views of the author based on Renee C. Rebman's personal experience, knowledge, and research. The information in this book serves as a general guide only. The author and publisher have used their best efforts in preparing this book and disclaim liability rising directly and indirectly from the use and application of this book.

Other Marshall Cavendish Offices:
Marshall Cavendish International (Asia) Private Limited, 1 New Industrial Road, Singapore 536196 • Marshall Cavendish International (Thailand) Co Ltd. 253 Asoke, 12th Flr, Sukhumvit 21 Road, Klongtoey Nua, Wattana, Bangkok 10110, Thailand • Marshall Cavendish (Malaysia) Sdn Bhd, Times Subang, Lot 46, Subang Hi-Tech Industrial Park, Batu Tiga, 40000 Shah Alam, Selangor Darul Ehsan, Malaysia

Marshall Cavendish is a trademark of Times Publishing Limited

All websites were available and accurate when this book was sent to press.

Library of Congress Cataloging-in-Publication Data
Rebman, Renee C., 1961-
  How do tornadoes form? / by Renee C. Rebman.
    p. cm. — (Tell me why, tell me how)
  Summary: "Provides comprehensive information on the process of tornadoes forming"—Provided by publisher.
  Includes index.
  ISBN 978-0-7614-4828-0
  1. Tornadoes—Juvenile literature. I. Title.
  QC955.2.R43 2011
  551.55'3—dc22
  2009041097

Photo research by Candlepants Incorporated

Cover Photo: Paul & Lindamarie Ambrose / Getty Images

The photographs in this book are used by permission and through the courtesy of:
*Getty Images*: Eric Meola, 1; Carsten Peter, 4; Ryan McGinnis, 5; Stephen Frink, 6; Frank Oberle, 11; Jon Van de Grift/Visuals Unlimited, Inc., 12; Steve Pope, 13; Stan Osolinski, 19; Kay Chernush, 21. *Photo Researchers Inc.*: Gary Hincks, 8, 9; Jim Reed, 22; Larry Miller, 24. *Alamy Images*: Ryan McGinnis, 10; A. T. Willett, 16, 17; Dennis MacDonald, 20. *Marshall Cavendish Image Library*: 14.

Editor: Joy Bean
Publisher: Michelle Bisson
Art Director: Anahid Hamparian
Series Designer: Alex Ferrari

Printed in Malaysia (T)
1 3 5 6 4 2

# CONTENTS

The distinctive funnel
shape of a tornado can
be seen from far away.

# What Is a Tornado?

Tornadoes are spinning, **funnel**-shaped masses of wind. They are as fascinating as they are frightening. Tornadoes form in powerful storm clouds and then stretch down toward land. Some tornadoes stop dozens of feet above the ground, where they can move along for miles. A true funnel-shaped tornado has a distinctive tail that touches the earth. Tornadoes that reach the ground are by far the most dangerous.

Tornadoes contain the fastest winds on Earth. The wind inside a tornado's swirling mass can reach more than 300 miles (483 kilometers) per hour. A tornado can also be huge in size. It can be as wide as several football fields and can suck up anything in its path.

A tornado can knock down trees, tear apart a house, and flip over cars and even trains as if they were toys. Pieces of broken objects called **debris** get caught in the

Tornado clouds can be huge, covering many miles.

5

strong, spinning winds and can be carried for hundreds of miles. Tornadoes are very unpredictable and do not always move in a straight path. Sometimes a tornado will come back to an area it has already crossed. It may even stay in one area without moving for a period of time. Most tornadoes last for less than fifteen minutes but can last for up to several hours.

Not all spinning masses of air are tornadoes. There are also **waterspouts** and **dust devils**. Waterspouts are whirling columns of air that form over lakes and oceans. They are smaller and weaker than tornadoes. They move across the water at a speed of about 10 to 15 miles (16 to 24 km) per hour. Waterspouts can suck fish out of the water and carry them miles

Waterspouts can form over any large body of water. They occur most frequently in the Florida Keys.

6

away. They can also damage ships. Ancient sailors mistakenly thought waterspouts were giant sea monsters.

Dust devils can form anywhere there is hot, dry land. They do not come from clouds. A strong wind picks up dirt and whirls it into a spinning mass much like wind picks up fallen leaves and spins them. A large dust devil can cause damage to land, buildings, and other property. Any sizable whirling air mass can be dangerous.

Since the beginning of time people have wondered about strange weather formations. They have tried to understand them and have also been frightened by them. Naturally, tornadoes cause much alarm. It was not until the 1950s that **meteorologists** connected tornadoes to particular types of cloud formations. They began to study how and when tornadoes form. Later, special technology such as **Doppler radar** became available. Meteorologists began to use this technology to help track possible tornadoes.

Learning more about tornadoes and how they occur is the only way to understand them and to try and prepare for them.

## Now I Know!

How long does the average tornado last?

Less than fifteen minutes.

This illustration shows warm air rising
and cooler air moving in the opposite
direction. This is the beginning of how a
tornado forms.

# A Twister Forms

Tornadoes are sometimes called twisters because of their twisting funnel. Funnel clouds form during powerful thunderstorms called **supercells**. Certain weather conditions have to be present for a supercell to happen. Most tornadoes occur during the late afternoon or early evening after the sun has heated up the atmosphere.

Before a storm, warm air on the ground begins to rise. This **updraft** sometimes meets a **downdraft** of cooler air that is moving in the opposite direction, pushing toward the earth. This is known as **wind shear**. The wind shear creates a spinning tube of air. The tube tilts upward into a vertical position as the updraft sucks up moisture from the ground and into the sky. High in the sky, the warm air cools and makes **condensation**— tiny droplets of water.

This illustration shows how warm air and cool air meeting can turn into a funnel of spinning air.

This condensation forms thunderclouds, which rise to between 30,000 and 50,000 feet (9,144 and 15,240 meters).

The spinning tube of air is lifted and trapped within the thundercloud as it continues to swirl. When a thunderstorm contains strong, lasting updrafts and rotating winds, it is called a supercell. The rotating winds are known as a **mesocyclone**. Sometimes a mesocyclone runs out of **humid** air and spins itself out. Only about half of the mesocyclones last long enough to produce tornadoes.

If a mesocyclone remains strong, it spins faster and faster, making a tight circle. Then it moves to the rear of the

This wall cloud is a sign that a tornado may form soon.

storm. This rotating section drops from the storm's base and is called a **wall cloud**. Wall clouds are a dangerous sign. Tornadoes drop down out of the wall cloud.

Before a tornado occurs, the sky can change to a gray-green color. There is usually a lot of lightning. Sometimes large **hail** pounds the earth. The hailstones are lumps of ice that can be as big as golf balls.

While the spinning air inside the tornado reaches great speeds, the speed at which a tornado moves along the ground is much slower. Most tornadoes move at about 10 to 20 miles (16 to 32 km) per hour.

The storm that takes place before a tornado touches down may produce hailstones, such as the ones in this picture.

Some tornadoes do not look like funnels at all. Some are shaped like a tube, and some like a wedge. Some are very fat, and some look skinny like a needle. Some have an hourglass shape. Most change shape right before they die out.

11

A tornado with a low rating on the
Fujita scale may still cause serious
damage, such as this home that lost
a wall during a tornado.

# Force of Destruction

The power and force of tornadoes are measured by the **Fujita scale**. It is named after the man who developed it: Theodore Fujita. He was a meteorologist who studied tornadoes. In 1951 he developed a scale based on the damage a tornado causes. The scale ranges from zero to six. It is the worldwide standard for rating tornadoes.

For example, an F0 tornado, the weakest on the scale, contains winds of 40 to 72 miles (64 to 116 km) per hour. It causes only light damage, such as tearing branches off trees or popping bricks off chimneys. An F2 tornado has winds of 111 to 135 miles (178 to 217 km) per hour. It can tear the roofs off of houses, uproot large trees, and overturn trains.

This building was wrecked by a tornado that ranks high on the Fujita scale.

F5 tornadoes are the strongest on record, with winds of 262 to 318 miles (422 to 512 km) per hour. An F5 tornado causes widespread damage. Houses are actually lifted off their foundations and carried away. Cars, boats, and farm machinery can be thrown miles from where they were parked. Fujita did include an F6 rating for tornadoes, with winds from 318 to 379 miles (512 to 610 km) per hour. Thankfully, an F6 tornado has never been recorded. Such a strong storm would destroy everything in its path.

Fujita also discovered other very important tornado facts. He was the first to realize that a single thunderstorm could make several tornadoes that would take off on their own separate paths. Fujita spent years studying tornado damage. He was interested in how tornadoes could destroy one room of a house and leave the next room untouched. What he discovered was amazing.

Fujita found out that inside a tornado funnel there were other smaller, whirling funnels he called **suction vortices**. These funnels suck up things in a looping pattern that leaves gaps just like a vacuum sweeper that passes over a carpet but leaves some dirt behind. This strange tornado behavior accounts for some true but incredible stories of items left standing undamaged in a room or home that is completely destroyed.

Famous tornado outbreaks that have been recorded are still being talked about and studied today.

Now I Know!

Which level of tornadoes are the strongest recorded?

F5 tornadoes.

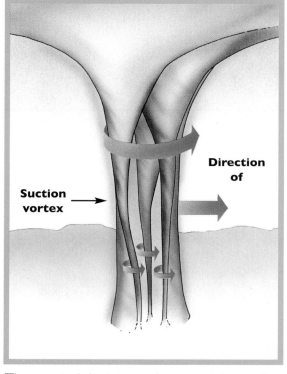

Suction vortex

Direction of

The most violent tornadoes contain smaller whirls within them.

The earliest recorded tornado in history occurred on October 23, 1091, in London, England. The roof of a church was torn off, and two men were killed.

Tragedy struck the American Midwest on April 3, 1974, when 148 tornadoes swept across several states. At one point fifteen tornadoes were on the ground at the same time. During the course of sixteen hours 335 people were killed. Xenia, Ohio, was the hardest-hit area.

This big tornado touched down
in Kansas.

# Tornado Alley

More than 1,200 tornadoes occur in the United States per year. This is more than anywhere else in the world. The midwestern portion of the United States has been given the name **Tornado Alley** because of the large number of tornadoes that occur in this area. It ranges from North Dakota down to Texas and spreads east to Ohio. The states in between include South Dakota, Nebraska, Kansas, Oklahoma, Louisiana, Iowa, Missouri, Illinois, and Indiana. The states in this area that

Oklahoma is hit by many tornadoes, such as this wedge shaped one.

experience the most tornadoes are Texas, Nebraska, Kansas, and Oklahoma.

This region is known as the Great Plains because it has large areas of flat land. Strong winds sweep across the plains. From March through June, people living in Tornado Alley are on the lookout for dangerous weather. Some states have more than six tornadoes a year. Kansas has more recorded F5 tornadoes than any other state.

The flat lands and fast-changing weather conditions contribute to the formation of strong storms. During the spring, the air in Tornado Alley is still cool and dry. Warm air flows up from the Gulf of Mexico bringing in moisture. As the moist air collides with the cooler air brought down from Canada, storms begin to form. This makes it the perfect condition for supercells.

By the summer, the air in Tornado Alley has warmed up and more closely matches the warm air sweeping up from the Gulf. The number of tornadoes decreases. Even then tornadoes can, and do, occur.

Tornadoes also happen frequently in other countries. Bangladesh, South Africa, Australia, Brazil, Canada, England, Italy, and France have numerous tornadoes per year. In fact, tornadoes have been reported on every continent except Antarctica, which does not have the cold- and warm-air contrast or the humidity needed for tornadoes to form.

It is hard to compare the number and strength of tornadoes in the United States with those in other countries. That is because recordkeeping methods are not the same. The use of the Fujita scale helps, yet records can still be inconsistent.

This tornado took place in the desert of Africa.

This Doppler radar station
is located in Virginia.

# Protection Against Danger

How can we protect ourselves against the dangers of tornadoes? Weather **forecasting** plays an important role. Meteorologists use Doppler radar to detect mesocyclones in the atmosphere. This method of forecasting tornadoes came into use in the early 1970s.

Doppler radar bounces beams off of water droplets inside of clouds. The beams can tell meteorologists whether the droplets are moving toward or away from the radar. Doppler

Meteorologists use Doppler radar to predict where storms will hit.

radar can also detect when the mesocyclone picks up speed as it spins faster and faster. Doppler radar can locate funnel clouds up to twenty-five minutes before they touch the ground. This early warning can help save lives. There is a nationwide Doppler radar network in the United States that helps forecast thunderstorms.

Some people actually go in search of tornadoes during a storm. They are known as storm chasers. Many storm chasers

This tornado researcher looks at the radar in his car, which is a storm chase vehicle.

are not meteorologists. But even nonprofessional storm chasers take their hobby seriously. They carry camcorders, tracking devices, radios, laptops, and other important pieces of equipment in their vehicles to relay information on what they find. Storm chasers are sometimes the first people to spot a tornado. Their photographs and videos help professionals study tornadoes.

When weather conditions are right to form a possible tornado, storm chasers drive toward the storm. They may only see an actual tornado once every ten or twenty times they go on a chase. Then they may have only a few minutes to set up their equipment and get recordings before they are forced to leave before the tornado gets too close.

If dangerous weather is detected or reported, meteorologists will send out warnings to the National Weather Service (NWS). The NWS then sends the warnings to radio and television stations. A tornado **watch** means weather conditions have developed that could favor the formation of a tornado. A **warning** means an actual tornado has been spotted on radar or by an eyewitness.

If there is a warning issued, people will be advised to seek shelter. The safest place to go during a tornado is the basement of your home or to an inside room with no windows. It is a good idea to take a battery-powered radio so you can listen to storm updates. It is also good to have thick blankets to cover yourself from flying debris.

If you are caught in a vehicle during a tornado, the driver should stop driving. Everyone in the car should leave the vehicle immediately and seek shelter. If there are no safe buildings nearby, you should lie facedown in a ditch and

Storm shelters are built to withstand the high winds of powerful storms such as tornadoes. This one is located in Kansas.

cover your head with your arms, staying as flat as you can.

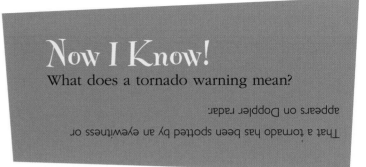

If there are storm shelters in your town, you can wait out the danger there. Storm shelters are buildings that have been built to hold up to strong winds. In Tornado Alley some communities have storm shelters for people to go to in the event of a tornado. Mobile home parks may have shelters available as well.

It is also good to have a tornado kit prepared in advance. Kits should include extra batteries for a radio, flashlights, blankets, canned food, and bottled water.

If a tornado does pass through your community, there are several important things to remember. Listen to the radio for instructions and information. Do not light matches or candles, as the flame could cause an explosion if there is a gas leak in the area. Stay away from any downed power lines, and do not go near any damaged buildings.

Tornadoes are a fact of life no matter where you live. They are an amazing example of nature's power.

# Activity

Here's your chance to make your own tornado. You can see what a spinning vortex looks like up close.

**The materials you will need are:**
- a clean, empty, 8-ounce jar
- clear liquid dish soap
- vinegar
- a small amount of glitter
- water

**What to do:**

1. Fill the jar with water until it is about three-quarters full.

2. Add 1 teaspoon of dish soap and 1 teaspoon of vinegar, then sprinkle in a pinch of glitter.

3. Close the jar tightly and then twist the jar in one direction. The water will be pulled along the glass

walls as you twist the jar. The fluid in the center will take longer to move. Keep twisting, and eventually all of the water will begin to spin. Now stop twisting the jar. The inside fluid will keep spinning. You will see a small "tornado" made up of spinning water and glitter for a few seconds. After the twister stops and all the glitter settles to the bottom of the jar, you can do it again. See if the speed with which you twist the jar determines how quickly a tornado forms. Count the seconds in order to see how long it takes for the tornado to stop.

This do-it-yourself tornado demonstrates how the spinning water picks up glitter just like the spinning air of a tornado picks up objects in its path. But this twister is safe and fun.

#  Glossary

**condensation—** The process by which water vapor forms tiny droplets of water. The water can take the form of fog, clouds, snow, or hail.

**debris—**Earth, broken pieces of buildings, tree limbs, and other items that get tossed around by tornadoes.

**Doppler radar—**A special type of radar that detects the direction and speed of wind.

**downdraft—**A downward current of air.

**dust devil—**A spinning mass of dusty air on the ground.

**forecasting—**Predicting what you think will happen to the weather.

**Fujita scale—**The scale that measures a tornado's intensity on a range from zero to six.

**funnel—**A long, thin, cone-shaped tube.

**hail—**A small ball of ice that drops from thunderclouds.

**humid—**Damp or moist.

**mesocyclone**—Spinning air inside a supercell that can produce a tornado.

**meteorologist**—A scientist who studies the weather.

**suction vortex**—Small whirling funnel inside a tornado.

**supercell**—A powerful thunderstorm.

**Tornado Alley**—The name given to the Midwest portion of the United States because of the large number of tornadoes the area has every year.

**updraft**—A current of rising air.

**wall cloud**—A cloud formation that hangs down from a supercell and can sometimes produce tornadoes.

**warning**—A weather alert given when a tornado is spotted on land or appears on radar.

**watch**—A weather alert indicating that conditions are right for producing a tornado.

**waterspout**—A funnel cloud that forms over the water.

**wind shear**—A change in wind speed or direction, or both combined.

# Find Out More

## BOOKS

Gibbons, Gail. *Tornadoes*. New York: Holiday House, 2009.

Olson, Nathan. *Tornadoes*. Mankato. MN: Capstone Press, 2006.

Oxlade, Chris. *Do Tornados Spin?* (Why Why Why). Broomall, PA: Mason Crest
 Publishers, 2009.

Sood, Malini. *Hurricanes and Tornadoes*. New York: PowerKids Press, Rosen
 Publishing Group, 2008.

Woods, Michael, and Mary B. Woods. *Tornadoes*. Minneapolis, MN: Lerner
 Publications Company, 2007.

## WEBSITES

Federal Emergency Management Agency: Tornadoes
www.fema.gov/kids/tornado.htm

Weather Wiz Kids: Tornadoes
www.weatherwizkids.com/weather-tornado.htm

Information about tornadoes from a storm chaser
http://skydiary.com/kids/tornadoes.html

Tornado Project Online
www.tornadoproject.com

# Index

Page numbers in **boldface** are illustrations.